VOTE
VOTE
VOTE

REDBACK publishing

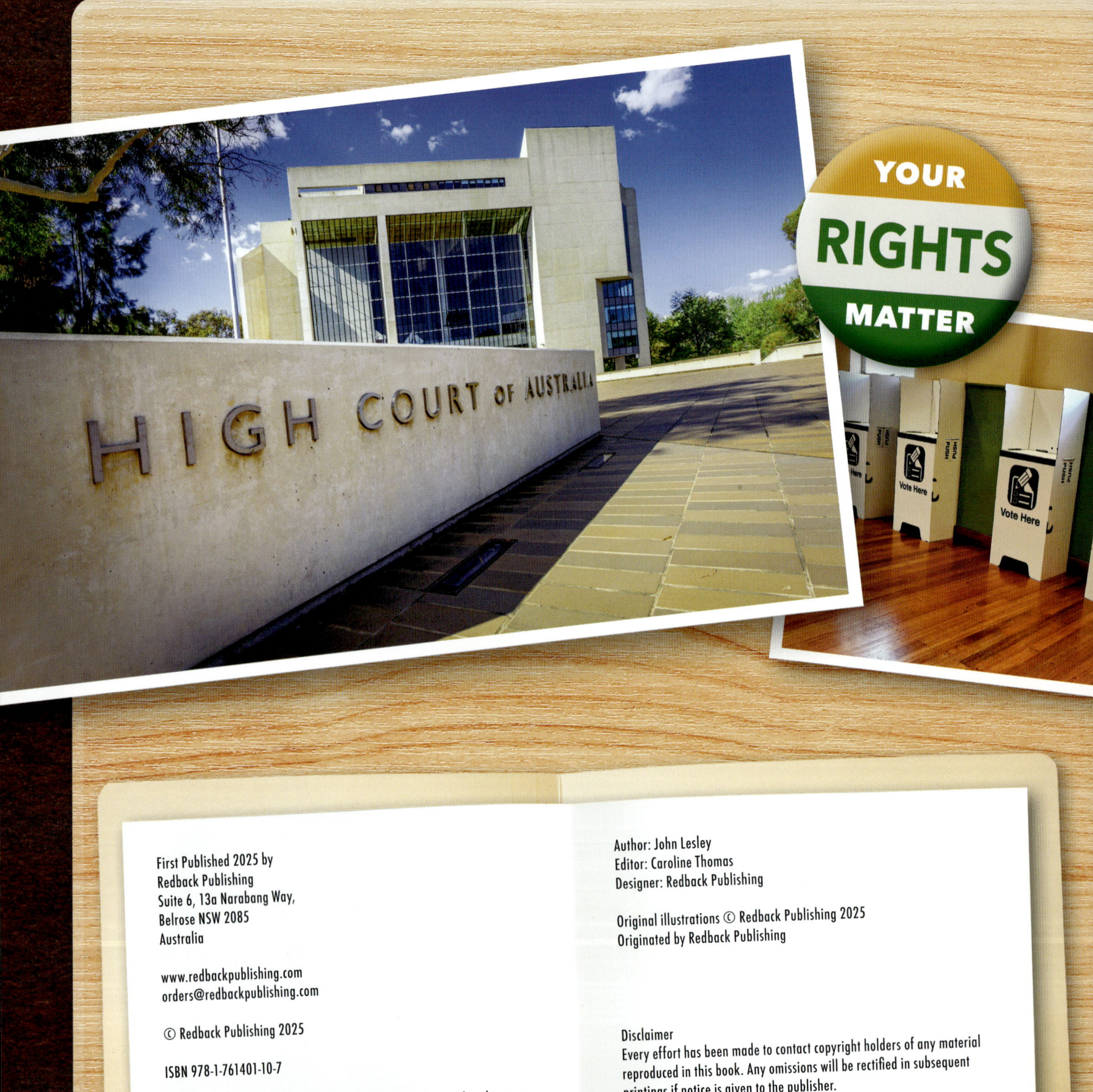

First Published 2025 by
Redback Publishing
Suite 6, 13a Narabang Way,
Belrose NSW 2085
Australia

www.redbackpublishing.com
orders@redbackpublishing.com

ISBN 978-1-761401-10-7

Author: John Lesley
Editor: Caroline Thomas
Designer: Redback Publishing

Original illustrations © Redback Publishing 2025
Originated by Redback Publishing

NATIONAL LIBRARY OF AUSTRALIA
A catalogue record for this book is available from the National Library of Australia

CONTENTS

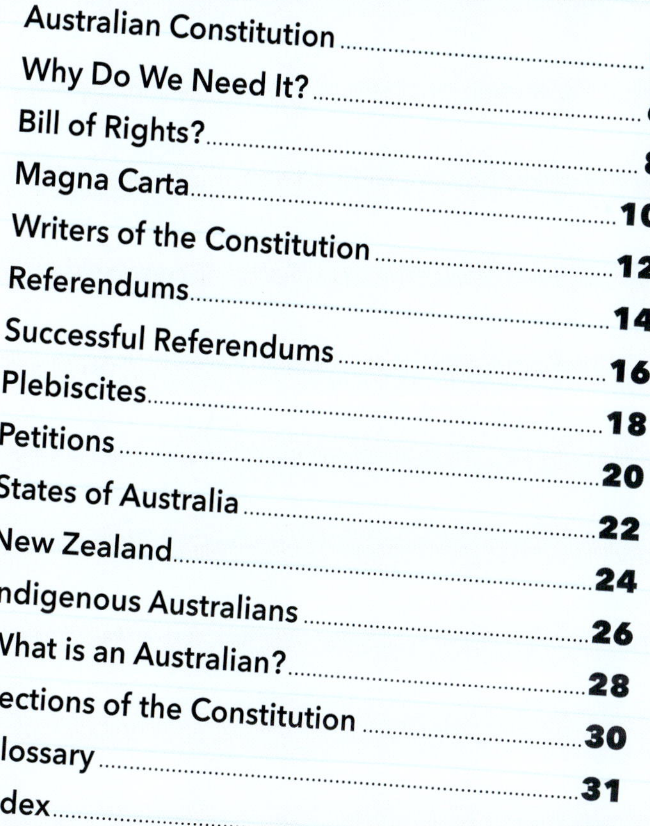

AUSTRALIAN CONSTITUTION

The Australian Constitution is the document that sets out how the Commonwealth of Australia should be governed.

The Constitution was written in the 1890s and became the Act of the British Parliament that resulted in the creation of the Commonwealth of Australia in 1901.

Commonwealth of Australia Constitution Act.

AN ACT

TO

Constitute the Commonwealth of Australia.

Cap. 12 [9th July 1900]

Democratic Foundations

The Constitution laid the foundations for the style of democratic government that Australia has today. It includes important citizenship rights, including freedom of religion, the right to trial by jury, and the right of citizens to vote for the people they want to represent them in Parliament.

Sir Henry Parkes

Charles Kingston

Sir Edmund Barton

Founding Fathers

What we now call the Australian Constitution began its existence as the Commonwealth of Australia Constitution Act. It was first proposed as a Bill that was drawn up by a group sometimes now referred to as the Founding Fathers.

Alfred Deakin

Andrew Inglis Clark

Sir Samuel Griffith

Queen Victoria

A United Country

The Commonwealth of Australia Constitution Bill hoped to legislate a union of the six separate Australian Colonies into a single Federation that could be governed as a united country. Australians voted at a number of referendums to decide whether they wanted an Australian Federation. They voted yes! Their permission to proceed led to a Bill being passed in each colony, and then an Act being signed and made into law by Queen Victoria of Britain in July 1900.

WHY DO WE NEED IT?

The main role of the Constitution is to define the way that the Australian government can operate. It does this by establishing the following political frameworks:

The Parliament

The law-making branch of government

The Executive Government

The Governor-General and the appointed Ministers who administer the operation of the laws

The Judicature

The High Court and other Federal courts that interpret the laws

Changing the Constitution

The Constitution makes it very clear that there is only one way that any part of it could be changed in the future. That process involves a referendum vote by the electors.

The States

The States of Australia exist as a result of the Constitution, which explains how they were to transition from being colonies, and what the rights of the State citizens are.

BILL OF RIGHTS?

A Guide for Lawmakers

A Bill of Rights is a document that is used in addition to a Constitution. It is used to guide the lawmakers of a nation and to set rules for how they are to make decisions for their citizens.

Australia has never had a Bill of Rights added to its Constitution. This is a matter which is under constant debate. The Founding Fathers and others believed Australia would be well protected by existing laws and by the content of the Constitution, and so they did not add a Bill of Rights. Today, some commentators disagree with that omission and believe that Australia needs its own Bill of Rights.

Australian States and Their Bill of Rights

A Bill of Rights is a statement of human rights. Some state and territory governments in Australia have passed human rights laws that now act as a Bill of Rights for their own citizens. These governments are those of the Australian Capital Territory, Queensland and Victoria.

Parliament of Victoria

The US Bill of Rights

We often hear the term Bill of Rights used, but how would it be used in Australia? The Bill of Rights for the citizens of the USA provides a good example of how one operates.

In 1789, the new US Congress made ten amendments to their nation's original Constitution. These amendments have become known as the Bill of Rights, now one of the most sacred documents in the United States. The Bill of Rights sets out the rights and privileges that belong to all United States citizens.

The French Declaration

During the French Revolution, the people executed their King and Queen before installing a new republic. In 1789, the revolutionaries created a guiding document for their actions and called it the Declaration of the Rights of Man and of the Citizen.

This document was important for both the creators of the US Bill of Rights, as well as the men who wrote the wording for Australia's own Constitution of 1901.

MAGNA CARTA

King John signs the Magna Carta

Basis for Laws

The original Magna Carta, (Latin for Great Charter), dates from 1215. It is a document detailing an agreement between the King of England and his barons, setting out their basic rights and emphasising the importance of the law. It shows the first, tentative steps towards representative government. The Magna Carta became the basis for all laws made in England, and it therefore influenced the creation of the Australian Constitution in 1901.

Historic Influence

The rights detailed in the Magna Carta also influenced the writers of the United States Declaration of Independence in 1776, as well as the United Nations Universal Declaration of Human Rights in 1948.

Australia's Copy

A copy of the Magna Carta from 1297 is on display at Parliament House in Canberra. It was acquired by the Australian Government in 1952. It is one of only four known to have survived. Because of its extreme age, the copy of the Magna Carta requires careful conservation to keep it in readable condition.

WRITERS OF THE CONSTITUTION

In writing the original Bill for the Constitution, the compilers referred to various sources from around the world, including the English Magna Carta of 1215, the British Bill of Rights of 1688, and the US Bill of Rights of 1789.

John Quick (1852 - 1932)

The idea to take the final decision about federation away from politicians and give it to the people to decide on is generally attributed to John Quick at the Corowa Conference in 1893. The matter had, of course, been discussed beforehand at previous meetings about a federation of the Australian colonies, but John Quick brought all the points together in a detailed document that allowed the process to move forward smoothly.

Henry Parkes (1815 - 1896)

Henry Parkes is called the Father of Federation because of the work he did to encourage the six separate colonies to join together and form a single nation. Henry Parkes gave a landmark speech on this subject in 1889. It is now called the Tenterfield Oration, and it is one of the most important speeches in Australia's history.

Edmund Barton (1849 - 1920)

Edmund Barton was born in Glebe, Sydney, and became a leading figure in the federation movement. Barton was elected to the New South Wales Parliament and was involved in drafting the Constitution for a future Commonwealth of Australia, but he will always be remembered as Australia's first Prime Minister, from 1901 to 1903. He later became a judge on Australia's first High Court.

REFERENDUMS

A Direct Vote

In modern Australia, a referendum is a direct vote by the Australian people to amend the Constitution. Australians can thank the compilers of the Australian Constitution for their foresight in adding the necessity of having a referendum of the people before any change is made to the Constitution. This is not the case in the United States, for example, where only politicians get to vote on constitutional change.

Australians are wary of changing their Constitution. There have been forty-five referendums in Australia from 1901 to 2023, but only eight have been passed by voters.

REFERENDUM RULES

Special rules apply when a referendum is held:

Double Majority

For a referendum to pass, a majority of citizens, plus at least four of the six States, need to agree to the change. This is called a double majority.

Saturdays Only

A referendum vote must be held on a Saturday.

Colonial Trailblazers

Before 1901 and the creation of the Australian Constitution, there had never been a referendum in any of the British colonies. Referendums were a rarity anywhere in the world in the late 1800s and had never been held in Britain itself either. The use of referendums by the six Australian colonies to decide whether to federate made them trailblazers.

Compulsory Age

Voting is compulsory in referendums for Australian citizens aged eighteen and over.

Final Decision

For a referendum to be held, Parliament needs to pass a Bill enabling it. Once the people vote at the referendum, their decision is final and cannot be changed by Parliament.

SUCCESSFUL REFERENDUMS

Of the forty-five referendums held in Australia from 1901-2023, these are the eight that received a 'Yes' vote and which resulted in amendments to the Constitution:

1906

To allow elections for both Houses of the Australian Parliament to be held at the same time.

1910

To give the Commonwealth power to take over debts of the States.

1928

To end Commonwealth payments to the States based on their population.

1946

To allow the Commonwealth the power to legislate on a wide range of social services.

1967

To allow Indigenous Australians to be included in the census, and give the Commonwealth government the power to make laws concerning them.

1977

To set the retirement age for Federal judges at seventy years

1977

To allow voters in Territories to vote in referendums.

1977

To be able to fill Senate vacancies mid-term with a person from the same political party.

The Senate

PLEBISCITES

In some countries, the word *plebiscite* means a referendum, but this is not the case in Australia, where the word has a different meaning. An Australian plebiscite has come to mean a vote by the people on a matter that will not result in any Constitutional change, although the two terms were used interchangeably in the early days of the Australian Federation.

1916 and again in 1917

On conscription of men to fight in the First World War.

1977

On a choice for the national song.

2016

On whether same-sex marriage should be legal.

Non-Binding Result

Regardless of how the people vote in a plebiscite, the government is not compelled to act on their decision. This contrasts with the results of a Federal referendum, which cannot be ignored.

Western Australia voted to leave the Commonwealth in 1933

State and Territory Plebiscites

Some Australian States and Territories have held a number of local plebiscites on matters that relate to their own jurisdictions.

Some plebiscite decisions could have made an enormous difference to Australian society if they had been allowed by Federal or State laws.

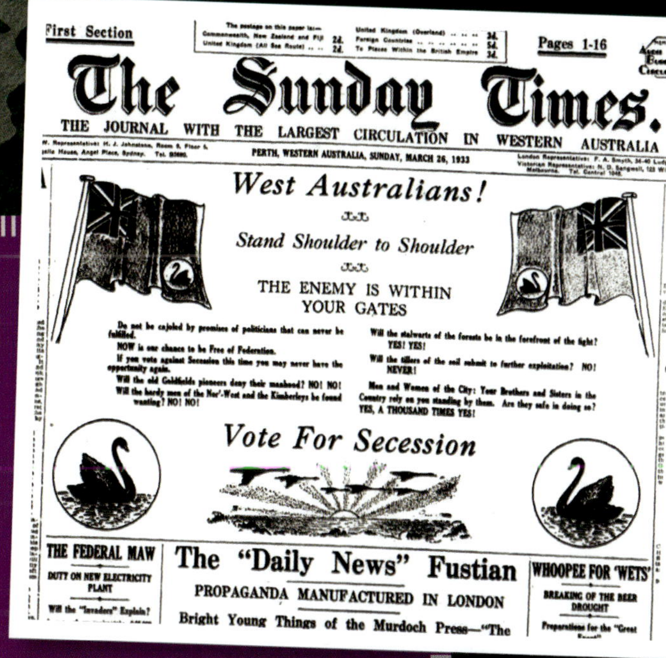

First Section

Pages 1-16

The Sunday Times.

THE JOURNAL WITH THE LARGEST CIRCULATION IN WESTERN AUSTRALIA

PERTH, WESTERN AUSTRALIA, SUNDAY, MARCH 26, 1933

West Australians!

Stand Shoulder to Shoulder

THE ENEMY IS WITHIN YOUR GATES

Do not be cajoled by promises of politicians that can never be fulfilled.

NOW is our chance to be Free of Federation.

If you vote against Secession this time you may never have the opportunity again.

Will the old Goldfields pioneers deny their manhood? NO! NO!

Will the hardy men of the Nor'-West and the Kimberleys be found wanting? NO! NO!

Will the stalwarts of the forests be in the forefront of the fight? YES! YES!

Will the tillers of the soil submit to further exploitation? NO! NEVER!

Men and Women of the City: Your Brothers and Sisters in the Country rely on you standing by them. Are they safe in doing so? YES, A THOUSAND TIMES YES!

Vote For Secession

THE FEDERAL MAW

DUTY ON NEW ELECTRICITY PLANT

Will the "Invaders" Explain?

The "Daily News" Fustian

PROPAGANDA MANUFACTURED IN LONDON

Bright Young Things of the Murdoch Press—"The

WHOOPEE FOR 'WETS'

BREAKING OF THE BEER DROUGHT

Preparations for the "Great

For example, in 1933 Western Australians voted to leave the Commonwealth and become an independent nation. However, it is not possible for any State to leave the Federation without a very lengthy process. A major hurdle to be overcome would be that the Constitution says the Federation of Australian States is "indissoluble", which means it cannot be broken apart.

PETITIONS

A petition is a formal request that can be made to one of the Houses of Parliament by an Australian citizen or a corporation.

The petition can be from just one person, or it may have thousands of signatures included with it which means that all those people agree with the request that is being made.

Purposes

Petitions may represent the opinions of large groups of voters. Petitions can also be about an injustice that a person feels they have suffered, or they can be about a government decision that a group of people think is unfair or will result in unintended negative outcomes for the community.

A bark painting from Yirrkala

Yirrkala Bark Petitions

In 1963, the Yolngu people of northern Australia presented the Australian Government with a petition asking for the return of their lands to them. The petition was written on bark in both English and Yolngu, using natural ochres as well as ink. Just like the Magna Carta, the Yirrkala Bark Petitions were signed by the leaders of the people with grievances about injustices that they were experiencing.

Yirrkala mural honouring Aboriginal land right leader Roy Dadaynga Marika MBE

STATES OF AUSTRALIA

The States of Australia exist as a result of the Constitution, which explains how they were to transition from being colonies, and what the rights of the citizens of the new States created should be.

Western Australia

The Constitution divided law-making powers between the new states and the new national parliament

One Federation

The six colonies of New South Wales, Queensland, South Australia, Tasmania, Victoria and Western Australia all had to approve the idea of joining together to form one federation. They had to give up some individual rights as a result, but in return, they gained protection from a large national defence force, as well as nationwide rules on immigration.

Melbourne children in fancy dress celebrate Federation in 1901

NEW ZEALAND

The Colony of New Zealand seriously considered joining the Commonwealth of Australia in 1901. The Australian Constitution defines the States as follows:

"The States shall mean … the colonies of New South Wales, New Zealand, Queensland, Tasmania, Victoria, Western Australia, and South Australia"

These publications were used by the Royal Commission to investigate if New Zealand should join the Commonwealth of Australia in 1901.

Gains and Losses

If New Zealand had decided to join the Commonwealth of Australia in 1901, it would have given up its rights to have its own defence force, to mint its own currency, or to collect income taxes. In return, it would have had various payments made to it by the Commonwealth, as well as all the rights and protections that the Australian States have today.

Royal Commission

New Zealanders set up a Royal Commission to investigate whether they should join or not. One of the commission's findings was that ordinary people knew very little about what joining the Commonwealth of Australia would mean for New Zealand.

A major problem was that Indigenous people would not be included as voters in the new Commonwealth, and so *"...the exclusion of the Maories would be a great injustice to them".*

INDIGENOUS AUSTRALIANS

Discriminatory

When the Australian Constitution was first written, it included some sections that were discriminatory against Aboriginal and Torres Strait Islander people. The Constitution prevented them from being included in the census, and they also could not register on the Commonwealth electoral roll to vote.

State Laws

The new Constitution of 1901 prevented the Australian Government from making laws on behalf of Australia's Indigenous people. Instead, each State was made responsible for the Aboriginal people living there. This meant that each State treated Indigenous Australians differently, resulting in widespread discrimination.

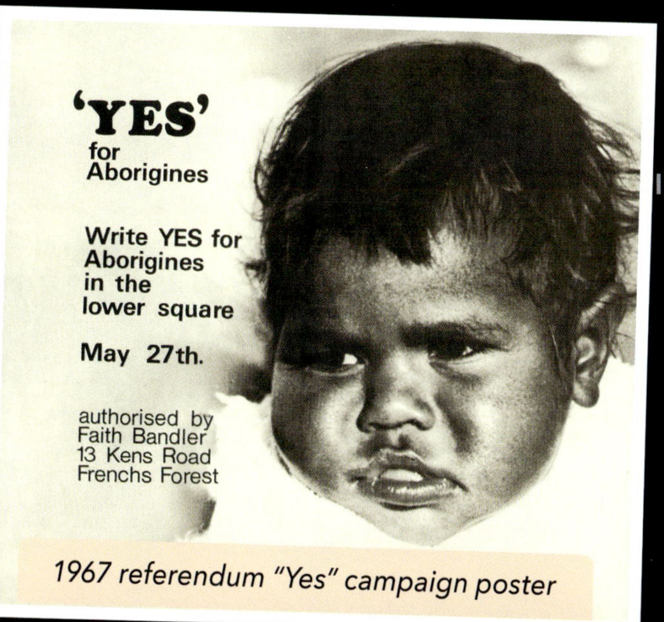

1967 referendum "Yes" campaign poster

Changing the Constitution

In 1967, the Australian people voted in a referendum to change parts of the Constitution concerning Aboriginal Australians. More than 90% of voters said 'Yes' to the proposed changes. This gave the Federal Parliament the right to make laws for Aboriginal Australians, and gave Aboriginal Australians the right to be included in the census.

The Voice Referendum

In October 2023, a referendum was held that asked voters to answer whether they approved of the following proposal:

"A proposed law: To alter the Constitution to recognise the First Peoples of Australia by establishing an Aboriginal and Torres Strait Islander Voice."

This referendum did not pass and was the forty-fifth one held in the Commonwealth of Australia.

WHAT IS AN AUSTRALIAN?

British Origins

The people writing the Constitution in the 1890s were British subjects, even though they also considered themselves Australians. They expected that the citizens of the new Commonwealth of Australia would remain British subjects. Although Australia would now have its own Parliament, it still had very close ties with Britain, and British culture was strong in Australia.

Australian Citizenship

Australian citizenship did not exist until 1948 when the Nationality and Citizenship Act created the first reference to an Australian citizen. The Constitution did not define citizenship of Australia. It allowed electors for the new Australian Parliament to be permitted to vote based on the existing laws of the States, which had a variety of racially based rules for colonial citizenship.

Holi and Harmony Day, Canberra

Undefined

Today, the Constitution does still not define who can be an Australian citizen, and therefore who can enrol to vote at government elections. This definition is in the Australian Citizenship Act 2007 (and its Amendments).

SECTIONS OF THE CONSTITUTION

Chapter I - The Parliament

- Part I – General
- Part II – The Senate
- Part III – The House of Representatives
- Part IV – Both Houses of the Parliament
- Part V – Powers of the Parliament

Chapter II – The Executive Government

Chapter III – The Judicature

Chapter IV – Finance and Trade

Chapter V – The States

Chapter VI – New States

Chapter VII – Miscellaneous

Chapter VIII – Alteration of the Constitution

The Upper House

The Lower House

GLOSSARY

amendment .... change (particularly to a law)

attributed to .... caused by

Bill .... proposal for a law

democratic .... relating to democracy

discriminatory .... showing discrimination

foresight .... knowing what will happen and planning for it

jurisdiction .... area within which a government has power

jury .... group of citizens who decide guilt or innocence at a trial in a court

mint (*verb*) .... make coins

privileges .... rights and advantages

tentative .... hesitant

trailblazer .... being the first to do something worthwhile

INDEX

Acknowledgements
Abbreviations: l–left, r–right, b–bottom, t–top, c–centre, m–middle

We would like to thank the following for permission to reproduce photographs (images © Shutterstock unless otherwise stated): p2tl Greg Brave/Shutterstock.com, p3t MM_photos/Shutterstock.com, p3bl Tom Roberts. Public domain. via Wikimedia Commons, p4cr National Archives of Australia, Public domain, via Wikimedia Commons, p5tl Eminent citizens [of] New South Wales, 1850-1900, Public domain, via Wikimedia Commons, p5tc The Swiss Studios, Melbourne, Public domain, via Wikimedia Commons, p5tr Swiss Studios, Public domain, via Wikimedia Commons, p6ml The Swiss Studios, Public domain, via Wikimedia Commons, p6mc Vandyck Photographers, Public domain, via Wikimedia Commons, p6mr https://nla.gov.au/nla.obj-136699298-v Public domain, via Wikimedia Commons, p6bl Bertha Müller, Public domain, via Wikimedia Commons, p6tl Greg Brave/Shutterstock.com, p6bl FiledIMAGE/Shutterstock.com, p8br FiledIMAGE/Shutterstock.com, p9tr 1st United States Congress, Public domain, via Wikimedia Commons, p9mr US Mint, Public domain, via Wikimedia Commons, p9bl neftali/Shutterstock.com, p10tl Arthur C. Michael (d. 1945), Public domain, via Wikimedia Commons, p11br nspeximus issue of Magna Carta, 1297., Parliament House Art Collection, Department of Parliamentary Services, Canberra ACT, p12tl National Archives of Australia, Public domain, via Wikimedia Commons, p12c Fairfax Corporation, Public domain, via Wikimedia Commons, p13bl State Library of New South Wales, Public domain, via Wikimedia Commons, p13tr Henry Walter Barnett, Public domain, via Wikimedia Commons, p15tl Contributor(s): Queenslander (Brisbane, Qld.: 1866-1939), Public domain, via Wikimedia Commons, p15tr Turner and Henderson, Public domain, via Wikimedia Commons, p16bc Donlawath S/Shutterstock.com, p17bl: EQRoyShutterstock.com, p18tl Reinforcement Referendum CouncilSands & McDougall Pty Ltd, Public domain, via Wikimedia Commons, p19br Western Press Limited, Public domain, via Wikimedia Commons, p21t Logic Images/Alamy Stock Photo, p21bl Ian Cochrane/Flickr, p22ml Tom Roberts. Public domain. via Wikimedia Commons, p23tr National Library of Australia from Canberra, Australia, No restrictions, via Wikimedia Commons, p24m Archives New Zealand from New Zealand, CC BY-SA 2.0 <https://creativecommons.org/licenses/by-sa/2.0>, via Wikimedia Commons, p25bl Yevgen Belich/Shutterstock.com, p27tl FelixFarley, CC BY-SA 4.0 <https://creativecommons.org/licenses/by-sa/4.0>, via Wikimedia Commons, p27bl Leanne Irwin/Shutterstock.com, p29ml Sasanan Trakansuebkul/Shutterstock.com, p29tr LittlePanda29/Shutterstock.com, p30mr ChameleonsEye/ Shutterstock.com, p30br FiledIMAGE/Shutterstock.com, p31b ChameleonsEve/Shutterctacknam

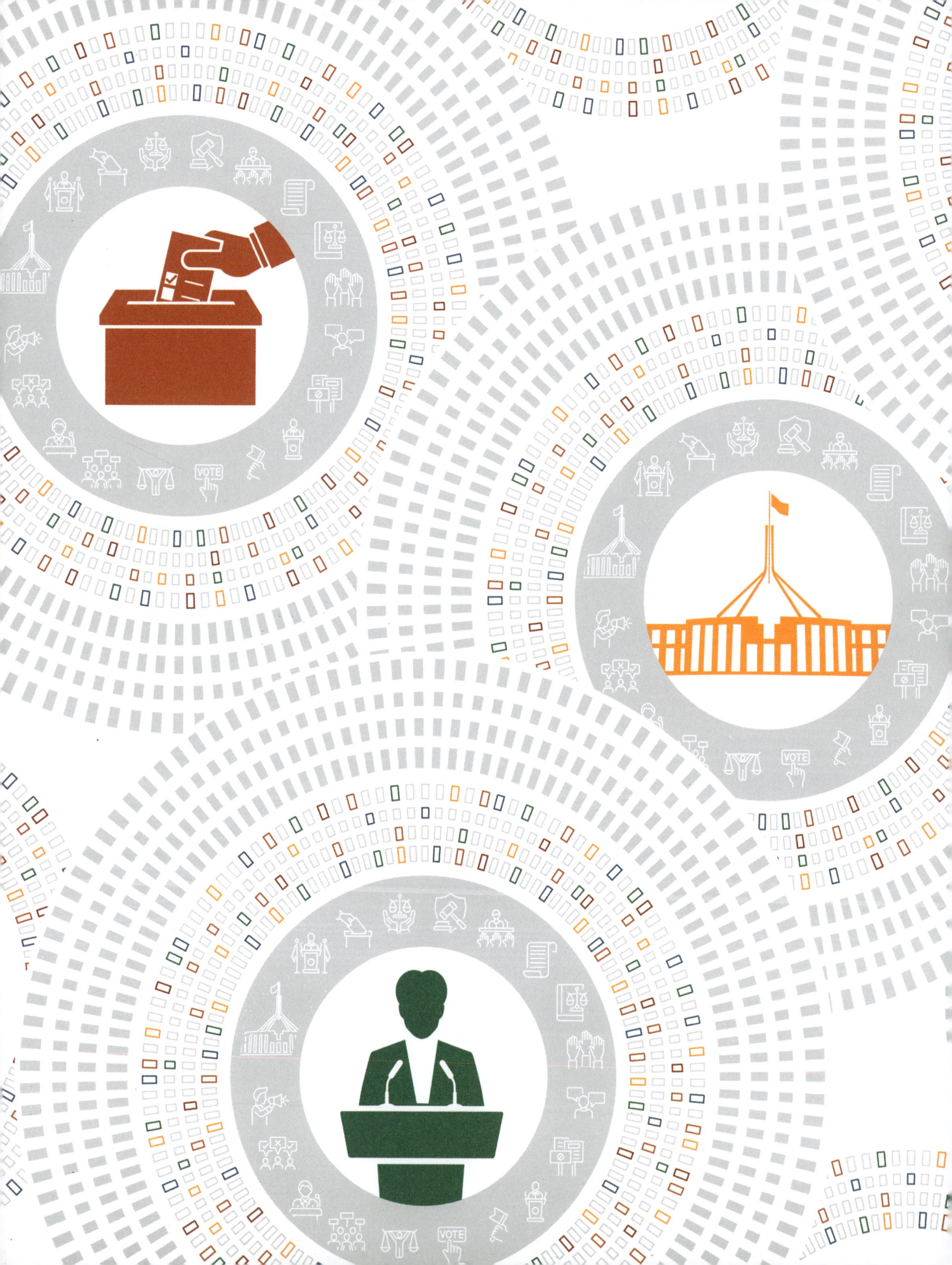

VOTE
VOTE
VOTE